MUSTANGS

AND

WILD HORSES

by Gail B. Stewart

Illustrated with photographs
by William Muñoz

Capstone Press
MINNEAPOLIS

Printed in the United States of America.

Capstone Press • 2440 Fernbrook Lane • Minneapolis, MN 55447

Editorial Director   John Coughlan
Managing Editor   Tom Streissguth
Production Editor   Jim Stapleton
Book Designer   Timothy Halldin

Library of Congress Cataloging-in-Publication Data

Stewart, Gail, 1949-
  Mustangs and wild horses / Gail B. Stewart; illustrated with photographs by William Muñoz.
     p. cm.
  Includes bibliographical references and index.
  Summary: A brief history and description of the wild horses of the western United States.
  ISBN 1-56065-301-9
  1. Mustang--West (U.S.)--Juvenile literature. 2. Wild horses--West (U.S.)--Juvenile literature. [1. Mustang. 2. Horses.] I. Muñoz, William, ill. II. Title.
  SF293.M9S73   1996
  599.7'25--dc20   95-11251
                                                    CIP
                                                    AC

00 99 98 97 96   8 7 6 5 4 3 2 1

Table of Contents

Quick Facts about Mustangs and Wild Horses 5

Chapter 1 Wild Horses of the West 7

Chapter 2 The Beginnings of the Wild Horse ...13

Chapter 3 Trouble for the Wild Horses 21

Chapter 4 Mustang Life 31

Chapter 5 The Mustang in Today's World 39

Glossary 45

To Learn More 46

Some Useful Addresses 47

Index 48

Quick Facts about Wild Horses

Description

Weight:
: Wild horses can weigh as little as 650 pounds (295 kilograms); **stallions** (male horses) weigh as much as 1,000 pounds (454 kilograms).

Physical features:
: Some wild horses have zebra-like stripes on their front legs, or a dorsal stripe on their backs.

Colors:
: Most are reddish-brown, with black manes, tails, and lower legs. Black, gray, and yellowish brown are other common colors.

Development

History of breed:
: Wild horses descend from horses brought by the Spanish to North America. During the settlement of the West, many of these animals escaped or were released into the wild.

Range

An estimated 45,000 wild horses live in western North America, especially Montana, Utah, and Nevada.

Chapter 1

Wild Horses of the West

The horses paw the ground, kicking up clouds of yellow dust. Snorting and whinnying, they rear up on their hind legs and pretend to fight. Nearby, on a small rise, several more horses stand as still as statues. Only their ears and eyes move as they listen and watch for danger.

Suddenly they hear the sound of men's voices carried by the wind. The horses quickly wheel and bolt into the hills. They disappear

A wild horse keeps its distance from humans.

The open grasslands of the West provide wild horses with food.

with a pounding of hooves and a wave of their long manes.

A Sight Like No Other

Tens of thousands of wild horses live in the western United States. Most inhabit Montana and northern Nevada. The horses are not easy to find. Those who have caught a glimpse of them are glad they did.

"It was amazing," says a woman who saw a large herd of horses in Montana. "I will remember the colors and the sounds all of my life. These are horses, but they're not the kind of horses I'm used to seeing."

Another woman agrees. "I wasn't sure what to expect. Just seeing these horses was a thrill, a sight like no other. They are like ghost horses from another era!"

A Confusing Name

People marvel at the beauty and spirit of the wild horses of the West. But the history of the wild horse also includes violence and cruelty. In the past 100 years, humans have shot and poisoned millions of these horses.

There are many mysteries about wild horses. Where did they come from? How did they live for centuries without help from humans? And how did these horses become the enemies of so many people?

Chapter 2

The Beginnings of the Wild Horse

All horses were once wild. About 55 million years ago, the ancestors of today's horses roamed North America. Scientists call this prehistoric horse **Eohippus**. This animal was more like a dog than a modern horse. It stood between 10 and 20 inches (25 and 50 centimeters) high. It had toes on its feet instead of hooves. Its back was somewhat arched, like the back of a greyhound.

Over millions of years, horses developed that were more like modern horses. But, for some unknown reason, horses disappeared from North America soon after the last Ice Age. About 8,000 years ago, there were no horses at all in North America. Where, then, did today's wild horses come from?

Coming to the New World

In the 15th and 16th centuries, Spanish explorers came to North America. They brought with them all the things necessary to

A stocky build is unusual for a wild horse. Most are thin compared to domesticated horses.

Horses that were set loose roamed the high plains and valleys of the Rocky Mountains.

settle in the New World. One of their most important possessions was the horse.

With their horses, the Spanish hauled heavy loads of supplies and tended the large cattle ranches they established. They also used their fast horses to conquer the Native Americans, who had no horses.

The Spanish horses thrived in the New World. The prairie grass was like a green sea of food that went on forever. Cold streams provided plenty of water. Conditions were so good that the number of horses doubled every fifteen months!

The early wild horses of the West grazed on a vast sea of grass and wildflowers.

The Mestenos

It is not surprising that some of the horses escaped and ran loose. The Spanish explorers did not concern themselves about the loss of a few runaways. These horses became known as **mustangs**, from the Spanish word *mestenos*, meaning "stray animals."

The Indians captured and bred the mustangs. They used the horses in battle and for hunting buffalo. Horses, especially the spotted horses known as **pintos**, became a valuable item of trade among Native Americans.

Over the years, the number of mustangs increased. When settlers from other parts of Europe came to North America, they brought horses that were different from the small, quick Spanish breeds. Some were tall, graceful **Thoroughbreds** from England and Ireland. Others were large, muscular horses used for hauling heavy loads. Still others were a mixture of breeds.

In time, some of these horses escaped or were turned loose by their owners. They joined

The mestenos had to have quick reactions and
endurance to survive in the wild. Mountain lions and
wolves were their natural enemies.

the wild mustangs and mated with them. Their young offspring roamed the plains with their parents. The herds that had once been made up of Spanish horses were now made up of hybrids—mixtures of several different breeds.

Strictly speaking, these horses were no longer the pure Spanish mustangs. But people still used that word when referring to the wild horses.

Millions of Horses

New horses joined the mustang herds over the years. Some had been turned loose by ranchers. Some had belonged to Indians who had been forced onto reservations. By the end of the 19th century, there were between 2 and 4 million wild horses running free throughout the West.

Chapter 3

Trouble for the Wild Horses

For many years, the mustangs flourished. Anyone who could capture them and tame them had a good supply of horses. They were fast, hardy, and strong, and they cost nothing.

Ranchers and cowboys used the mustangs to tend cattle. Trappers and fur traders also put them to work. During the Civil War (1861-1865), soldiers rounded them up for military service. The army of the North needed 200,000 horses each year for its troops.

Nothing but a Nuisance

By the beginning of the 20th century, the herds had become a problem. Ranchers were buying and fencing land throughout the West. The huge herds of wild horses were fighting the ranchers for grazing land.

"Ranchers felt the horses were nothing but a nuisance," says one Nevada rancher who remembers his father complaining about them. "They ate twice as much as cattle, and their sharp hooves cut into the land and uprooted the grass. To a rancher, grazing land is as precious as gold, and the horses were ruining it."

The ranchers handled the problem in several different ways. Some drove the horses from the grazing lands and built sturdy fences to keep them out. Others tried to kill as many of the horses as possible.

Two black mustangs splash across a western water hole.

Whenever these ranchers saw a wild horse, they tried to shoot it. Some ranchers poisoned waterholes where they knew mustangs gathered to drink. In Utah, where the herds were very large, ranchers killed thousands of horses by

stampeding them over cliffs near the Colorado River.

In the 1940s, the killing of wild horses was at an all-time high. To make matters worse, pet-food companies were buying horsemeat.

They paid between $10 and $20 for each mustang delivered to their factories.

There were plenty of people willing to capture horses for this purpose. Some used low-flying airplanes to chase the horses. After running for many miles, the frightened horses became too tired to run any more. Men called "mustangers" then loaded them into holding pens. The horses were forced into trucks and shipped to the pet-food factories.

A Friend for the Wild Horses

A woman named Velma Johnston, who lived near Reno, Nevada, saw truckloads of wild horses on their way to market. She was upset by the sight of hot, sweaty horses trying desperately to breathe in the cramped trucks.

Johnston and her husband watched as mustangers chased the horses. She saw the men tie heavy tires around the horses' legs to prevent them from running or kicking. She sent photographs of the suffering mustangs to newspapers and magazines.

A wild horse stays watchful, even while at rest.

At first, the mustangers laughed at her. Then they began to worry. They made a lot of money by capturing and selling the wild horses. They didn't want anything to upset their business. Some threatened her with guns. But she kept on following their trucks.

Laws to Help

Velma Johnston worked hard to bring the sad story of the mustang to the public's attention. She begged the government to do something to protect the horses. She talked to humane societies and to county sheriffs. She

Most wild horses run on the large tracts of public lands that still exist in the western United States.

organized a huge letter-writing campaign among schoolchildren.

The officials did not take her seriously. They called her "Wild Horse Annie" behind her back. When she proposed a law that would make it illegal to use airplanes and vehicles to herd the horses, lawmakers ignored her. But when letters by the thousand came pouring in, they decided to do something.

One congressman from Nevada said, "Am I going to be influenced by a bunch of children? Am I going to support this bill because kids— mine and others—are sentimental about ponies? You bet your boots I am!"

The law, sometimes called The Wild Annie Bill, was passed. It was followed in 1971 with a tougher law. No longer could people capture, hunt, or kill the mustangs. Thanks to Velma Johnston and other concerned citizens, the wild horses of the West were saved.

Chapter 4
Mustang Life

To people who think they know a lot about horses, wild horses can be surprising. They differ in many ways from **domestic** horses.

"It is truly amazing what these horses are capable of," says one man who has studied mustangs for many years. "If you think that horses cannot live without someone pumping water for them, or pitching hay for them, or building them warm stables, guess again."

A Different Look

Wild horses are smaller than most domestic horses. A wild stallion is considered large if it

Life on the slopes of the Rockies has made the wild horse a sturdy specimen.

weighs 1,000 pounds (454 kilograms). A Thoroughbred stallion usually weighs about 1,200 pounds (545 kilograms).

When people see a mustang for the first time, they are surprised at how thin the horse seems. Often, they can even see the horse's ribs. Unlike domestic horses, wild horses must work hard to find enough grass to eat. A healthy mustang can weigh as little as 650 pounds (295 kilograms).

Wild horses come in many colors. The most common is reddish-brown, with a black mane, tail, and lower legs. Black, gray, and yellowish-brown horses are common, too. Some wild horses—including pintos and **Appaloosas**—have patterns. Appaloosas have a white area with little dark blotches on their rump.

Some wild horses have the same markings as ancient horses. These include zebra-type stripes on the front legs or a long stripe, called a **dorsal stripe**, that runs down the back.

Family Bands

In the wild, horses live in small groups called family bands. A band is made up of a stallion and his group of mares, or female horses. Some stallions have just one mare, while others have as many as 15 or 20. Also included in the family band are the young horses, called foals. Foals live in the family band until they are two or three years old.

The stallion is the protector of the band. He has to be ready to defend his mares from other stallions, who will wait for a chance to steal them. Most stallions bear the scars of many such battles.

There are other dangers that stallions must face. Mountain lions may attack a young or

A mother mustang guards her young foal.

The dust flies as rival mustang stallions battle.

injured horse. Wolves are another enemy. The
biggest threat to wild horses, however, has
always been humans.

When he senses danger, a stallion snorts a
warning. His family knows that it is time to
run, and run quickly. One of the mares leads
the way, while the stallion stays behind to
make sure that even the smallest foal gets away
safely.

Keen Instincts

Life in the wild is tough, and only the strongest and hardiest horses will survive. Over many generations, wild horses have developed keen instincts—instincts that domestic horses do not have.

"Wild horses have an amazing ability to adapt," says one horse expert. "Life is hard in the desert—the summer sun sizzles and, in the winter, temperatures get below zero. Horses might have to go for days between drinks of water, and grazing land is hard to find. A domestic horse would get weak or sick. But these mustangs thrive!"

For instance, mustangs can smell water holes as far as 60 miles away. They can detect an approaching enemy by a distant, faint smell carried on a breeze. They can also use their sensitive hooves to feel the vibration of another animal through the ground.

Wild horses are also incredibly fast. "They may or may not be able to beat a racehorse on a nice level track," says one expert. "But on the rocky, uneven ground of the desert and

Mares and their foals stay together for several years in the family bands.

hillsides, they fly. Even a lame mustang could outrun a racehorse on open terrain."

Chapter 5

The Mustang in Today's World

The wild horses of the West have been protected by law since 1971. No one can kill them, sell them, or endanger them.

Because humans are no longer a threat, the number of wild horses has increased. In 1970 there were fewer than 10,000 wild horses. Twenty-five years later, the population is about 45,000. These animals are no longer threatened by extinction.

But the growing herds of wild horses have created new problems. The vast public lands where the herds live is also used by ranchers for grazing land. There is not enough grass or

Many wild horses have settled down to life on a ranch.

water to support the wild horses as well as the cattle and sheep that the ranchers own.

What Can Be Done?

No one wants to see the slaughter of the wild horses that took place in the past. But most people realize that there are too many wild horses. Experts say that a herd of 30,000 would not overgraze the lands.

But how should the herd sizes be reduced? Some people believe that it would be best to "thin" the herds by killing some of the horses. Other people have protested this plan. They say that there are better ways to deal with the extra horses.

Adopt-a-Horse

One successful plan is called Adopt-a-Horse. Workers for the Bureau of Land Management (BLM), a government agency, capture the horses. The bureau offers them to the public for $125 each.

Some of the horses are easy to sell. They are healthy and beautiful, and they can learn to trust people. Fifteen-year-old Dana adopted a gray mustang that she named Tony.

"I was a little nervous at first," she says. "I didn't know what to expect—I guess I thought he'd be kicking and bucking like crazy. But he turned out to be pretty gentle. I worked hard to earn his trust, and we are friends now."

Wild horses graze on a fenced western pasture.

The Unwanted Horses

But there are some horses that the bureau knows won't be adopted. Some are not as beautiful as the other horses. Some are too old, and some are too wild to ride.

For years, the BLM kept these horses in holding pens and corrals. It was expensive and, some say, cruel. In 1988 some landowners offered to rent parts of their land to the BLM for the horses. Operating these natural **refuges** is less expensive than keeping the horses in corrals, and it is better for the horses.

Another plan has helped turn some of the "unwanted" horses into "wanted" horses. The program sent some of the wildest horses to prisons, where inmates helped tame the animals. This program made the horses more trusting of humans. It has also helped many prisoners learn valuable skills like discipline and patience.

Free Forever?

There are thousands of wild horses roaming the deserts and plains of the West. They have caused problems for some people, especially ranchers. They have endured cruel treatment from humans and from nature.

The issue of wild horses is still controversial. "The refuges are great for the horses, but still expensive," says one expert. "No one knows how long the government can afford to keep spending money on the wild horses."

Those who have worked hard to save the wild horses are confident that the problems can be solved. "These horses have endured a lot, but they're still here" says one BLM worker. "There is a lot of heart in these horses, a strong will to survive. People in the United States will be arguing about how to pay for their upkeep. It will be a political issue, with lots of angry words on both sides. But the horses will live on, adapting to any hardship we throw at them. It's the only way they know."

Cooperation between ranchers and government agencies may help the wild horses to survive.

Glossary

Appaloosa—a speckled horse, usually with egg-shaped spots on its rump

domestic—tamed by humans

dorsal stripe—a mark running down a horse's back

Eohippus—a prehistoric horse, related to the modern horse

foal—a young male or female horse

mare—a female horse more than four years old

mustang—horses living in the wild; originally a wild Spanish horse

pinto—a horse that has a pattern of spots on its coat

refuge—land set aside especially for wild horses

stallion—a male horse more than four years old

Thoroughbred—a tall, graceful horse bred originally in Northern Europe

To Learn More

Ancona, George. *Man and Mustang.* New York: Macmillan, 1992.

Beebe, B. F. and James R. Johnson, *American Wild Horses.* New York: David McKay and Co., 1964.

Featherly, Jay. *Mustangs: Wild Horses of the American West.* Minneapolis: Carolrhoda Books, 1986.

Green, Carl R. and William R. Sanford. *The Wild Horses.* Mankato, MN: Crestwood House, 1986.

Henry, Marguerite. *Album of Horses.* New York: Rand McNally, 1951.

Patent, Dorothy Hinshaw. *Where the Wild Horses Roam.* New York: Clarion Books, 1989.

Stewart, Gail B. *Cowboys in the Old West.* San Diego, CA: Lucent Books, 1995.

Some Useful Addresses

American Mustang Association
P.O. Box 338
Yucalpa, CA 92399

Canadian Wild Horse Society
3660 40th Street, S.E.
Salmon Arm, BC V1E 4M3

International Society for the Protection of Mustangs and Burros
6212 E. Sweetwater Avenue
Scottsdale, AZ 85254

Spanish Mustang Registry
Route 3, Box 7670
Willcox, AZ 85643

Index

Adopt-a-Horse, 41
Appaloosas, 33

buffalo, 17

cattle, 22
Civil War, 21
Colorado River, 25
cowboys, 21

domestic horses,
    31-33, 36
dorsal stripe, 33

Eohippus, 13
Europe, 17
explorers, 14-15,
    17

family bands, 33-
    35
fighting, 34
foals, 34

fur traders, 21

grass, 16, 33, 40
greyhounds, 13

humane societies,
    28
hybrids, 19

Ice Age, 14
instincts, 36

Johnston, Velma,
    26-29

mestenos, 17-19
Montana, 8-9
mountain lions, 35

Native Americans,
    15, 17
Nevada, 8, 29
North America,
    13-14

pintos, 17, 33
prisons, 43

ranches, 15
ranchers, 19, 21-
    22, 24-25, 40
refuges, 43

Spanish horses,
    13-17, 19

Thoroughbreds,
    17, 32
trappers, 21

water, 16, 36, 40
Wild Annie Bill,
    29
wolves, 35